For Clare McGrath,
with colossal love.
C.H.

For Mum,
with lots of love! xx
T.F.

First published in 2024 by Frances Lincoln Children's Books,
an imprint of The Quarto Group. 100 Cummings Center, Suite 265D, Beverly, MA
01915, USA.
T +1 978-282-9590 F +1 078-283-2742 www.Quarto.com

ISBN 978-0-7112-7875-2
eISBN 978-0-71127876-9
The illustrations were created with graphite and coloured pencil.
Set in Adobe Caslon Pro.

Published by Peter Marley. Edited by Helen Mortimer.
Art direction by Karissa Santos. Designed by Zoe Tucker and Sasha Moxon.
Production by Dawn Cameron.

Manufactured in Guangdong, China TT012024

1 3 5 7 9 8 6 4 2

FSC
www.fsc.org
MIX
Paper | Supporting
responsible forestry
FSC® C016973

COLOSSAL WORDS for KIDS

written by
COLETTE HILLER and illustrated by **TOR FREEMAN**

Frances Lincoln
Children's Books

Your word is your wand

There's a wonderful feeling in knowing precisely the right word for something. Like fitting in a piece of a jigsaw—it's hugely satisfying. *And* it helps you get straight to the point. Who'd ever want to say **second to last** when instead you could say . . . **penultimate!**

> "**Words are,** in my not-so-humble opinion, our most inexhaustible source of **magic.**"
>
> **Albus Dumbledore**
> *Harry Potter and the Deathly Hallows*
> by J. K. Rowling

The words in this book are **strong** and useful. Even the small ones are **mighty**. Some may look difficult at first—but don't be fooled. All these words are easy to use. What's more, you'll find that using them is **colossal fun!**

> "I like good **strong words** that **mean something.**"
>
> **Jo March**
> *Little Women* by Louisa May Alcott

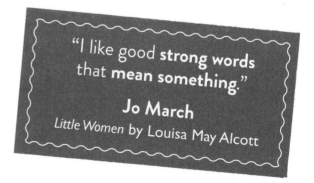

DEFINED IN RHYME TO STICK IN THE MIND

This book sets out to make the discovery of new words as glorious as the words discovered. Unlike a dictionary, the definitions aren't just told to you. Instead, the meanings will *unfold* for you, revealing themselves in entertaining ways. Each word is defined by way of a rhyme.* After reading it through, you'll feel able to use the word. It's a ready-to-use collection.

*Note: when a word has several meanings, the rhyme defines just one of them.

Hit the volume!

These poems are meant to be **read aloud** —even if nobody else is around! Doing this helps you remember the word. Plus, it's **fun**. Keep a steady beat. Try not to rush. And give any punchline a bit of a **punch!**

Start wherever you like

The alphabet starts with A, but **you** don't have to! Choose any word you like the sound of . . . and off you go!

"The difference between the almost right word and the right word is . . . the difference between the lightning bug and the lightning."

Mark Twain

Acquiesce

If you **acquiesce** to someone's request,
you give in and just say, **"Yes!"**
You don't protest
as it all seems best
to go with the flow
so you **acquiesce**.

Acrimonious

When a conversation
is not the least harmonious
but full of angry bitterness
we say it's **acrimonious**.

Adjective

If **adjectives** were not allowed
things could not be **straight** or **round**.
A cat could only be a cat—
it couldn't be **black** and couldn't be **fat**.
Nothing could ever be **hot** or **cold**,
and *you* could never be **young** or **old**.
You couldn't be **sweet**, you couldn't be **bad**,
and no one could ever be **happy** or **sad**.
If all these words were locked away—
it wouldn't be easy to know what to say.
But since we can use adjectives
we can describe how something is.
(Whew!)

"In writing. Don't use **adjectives** which
merely tell us how you want us to feel . . .
I mean instead of telling us the thing is 'terrible'
describe it so that we'll be terrified."

Letters to Children by C.S. Lewis

Alliteration

A group of grinning gremlins
is an excellent example.
Sixty singing Santas
is another super sample.

And so is **Vick the Vampire**
in Vancouver on vacation.
The repetition of a sound
is called **alliteration!**

ALL IN THE WORD

Alliteration tells you the sounds are **all** alike.
Tongue twisters are made of this device.
Try this fishy one:

Fresh fried fish; fried fish fresh

Ambiguous

"Matt, how do you like my hat?"
Pat asked her older brother.
"All I can say," said Matt, "is that
your hat is like no other!"

Was this in fact a compliment?
Did Matt think it was lovely?
But then again he might have meant
he thought her hat was ugly!

**When something is ambiguous
its meaning isn't clear.**
It's really up to you to choose
what you want to hear!

AMBIGUOUS

Rabbit or duck? Which is true?
It's **ambiguous** – it's up to you!

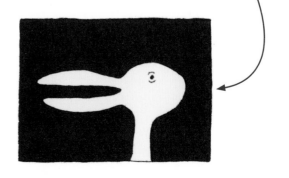

Bravado

Although his knees were trembling,
he spoke with great **bravado**.
"I'm not at all afraid to fight
a ten-foot avocado!

"I've done this kind of thing before,"
boasted young Ricardo.
But inside he was terrified
and feeling desperado.

In no way could he ever slay
a ten-foot avocado.
For he was just a flea, you see,
who boasted with **bravado**.

Brevity

When you speak with **brevity**,
you don't bang on and on.
You quickly make your point and you don't
faff or take too long.

When you *write* with **brevity**
the very same is true.
Why would you use **100** words
when **42** will do?

"**Brevity** is the soul of wit."
Hamlet by William Shakespeare

*These words were written hundreds
of years ago and are still true today.
Jokes are funnier when they are short.*

Buoyant

Lifting, airy, bouncy, brimming,

lightly springing up . . .

When something's **buoyant**,

up it goes and rises to the top.

A boat is **buoyant** (you would hope).

A person can be too.

A **buoyant** mood is happy

with a light and sunny view.

"There was a shrewd, **buoyant** air about him
as he sat up, looked round and rubbed both
front paws over his nose."

Watership Down by Richard Adams

Capacious

Something **capacious**

is roomy and is spacious

(but spacious is mainly for physical spaces).

A **capacious** mind

or bag . . . or pot

has the capacity to hold a lot!

"There is a **capacious** writing-table in the room on which is a pretty large accumulation of papers."
Bleak House by Charles Dickens

Chortle

A belly laugh is deep and long—
a titter, very short.
A **chortle** is a noisy kind of
chuckle with a snort.

Contrite

If you've done something wrong
that you know wasn't right
but you're ever so sorry
then you are contrite.

If you're *really* contrite,
there really can't be
any kind of **but** attached
to your apology!*

* I'm sorry but . . . isn't contrite.
It's just an excuse to insist you are right!

Deviate

Things to remember when you are baking:

Stick to the recipe that you are making.

Resist adding extras you think may be great.

Do as they tell you and don't **deviate**.

Things to remember when you are rhyming:

Think about rhythm and meter and timing.

Stick to a pattern and don't **deviate**

and suddenly go wondering off in an entirely unexpected direction.

Discombobulated

When you're **discombobulated**,
you're completely **muddled**.
You're **disturbed** and **agitated**.
You're extremely **puzzled**.

Say your mother suddenly
just turned into . . . a seal!
You'd be **discombobulated**.
That's how you would feel.

Or say one day, your dad became
a flying giant kettle.
You'd be **discombobulated**,
anxious, and **unsettled**.

When things are **topsy-turvy**
and you're totally **confused**,
discombobulated is
the *perfect* word to use!

Disingenuous

A thing that's **disingenuous**
is something that's **misleading**.
It isn't really genuine—
it's meant to be **deceiving**.

Something **disingenuous**
seems honest on the surface . . .
then leads you up the garden path
(which is its very purpose).

The wolf said to Red Riding Hood,
"You look so sweet m'dear."
But he was **disingenuous**.
That wolf was **insincere**!

For when he said that she looked sweet,
the thing he *didn't* mention
was she looked sweet enough to eat.
(And *that* was his intention!)

Doleful

Gloomy old Eeyore was stuck in a rut,
and Christopher Robin could not cheer him up.
He wished him good morning, but Eeyore looked glum.
"I suppose," he said moodily, "it's good for some.
But I've lost my tail, and I doubt I shall find it.
I don't complain—but don't think I don't mind it!
I see no reason why I should feel hopeful."
So gloomy old Eeyore went on looking **doleful**.

A GLOOMY NOTE

Eeyore is so famously gloomy that he's been turned into an adjective! Someone who is Eeyorish is extremely **doleful**!

Effervescent

It may sound complicated
but the fact is, it is not.
Say eff–er–ves–cent slowly.
You can hear the bubbles pop!
When something's effervescent,
it's not difficult to tell.
Some drinks are effervescent,
and some people are as well.
When somebody is bubbly
and sparkly and pleasant
and they fizz like Coca-Cola
you could say they're
effervescent!

Empathy

"I'm sorry for you" is sympathy.
"I *feel* your sorrow" is **empathy**.

Sympathy's pitying somebody else.
Empathy's feeling their feelings *yourself*.

**If you can imagine how it must be
to stand in *their* shoes: that's empathy.**

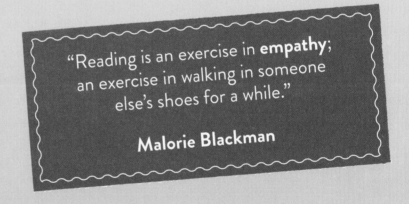

"Reading is an exercise in **empathy**;
an exercise in walking in someone
else's shoes for a while."

Malorie Blackman

Epiphany

A person can just suddenly
have a flash of clarity
that makes them see things differently.
And that is an epiphany.

You might wake up and understand
how heat makes molecules expand.
Or in a whoosh, you plainly see
a vet is what you're meant to be!

That crystal-clear discovery
arrives quite unexpectedly.
That moment of "Aha, I see!"
would be your own **epiphany**.

Isaac Newton's **epiphany**
was understanding gravity.

Fallible

Nobody is perfect.
We all can make mistakes.
Everyone is fallible.
We're *human* for Pete's Sake!

And so if you should try your best
but *still* you make an error,
the reason is you're fallible.
And *not* that you're not clever!

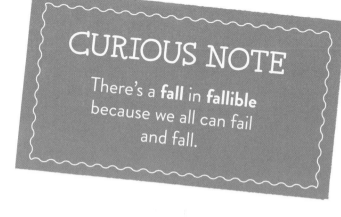

CURIOUS NOTE

There's a **fall** in **fallible** because we all can fail and fall.

"I'm in fine **fettle** and fired with a desire to paint."

Claude Monet

Fettle

To be in *fine* fettle
is a fine place to be.
You're thriving and doing
spectacularly.
There's no *dreadful* fettle.
There's just the one kind.
And that type of **fettle**
will always be fine.

Figment

A **figment** is a notion
made of thoughts alone.
There's nothing real about it yet
your head gives it a home.
A **figment**'s something you create—
a total fabrication.
The only place a **figment** lives
is your imagination.

CURIOUS NOTE

Figment and **finger** come
from the same Latin root
fingere, which means to
shape or form. In the same
fi family is **fiction**: a shaped
or invented story.

Garrulous

Someone who is **garrulous**
is chatty, that's for sure.
They talk at length about dull things . . .
And then they talk some more.

Their babble's always trivial
yet on and on they go . . .
(When somebody is **garrulous**
alas, they do not know!)

Gawping

"Cinderella!"
cried the prince,
"Oh, won't you marry me?"
And the stepsisters stared
open-mouthed . . .
GAWPIng
stupidly.

Gregarious

Gregory was a **gregarious** guy:
outgoing, sociable, not at all shy.
He liked a good party and loved a good chat.
Gregarious Greg was a natural at that.

Harried

Harry is late.
He's off to get married.
Harry is *hurried*
and *worried* . . .
He's **HARRIED!**

"His face suddenly had become tight and white and **harried**."

I Conquered by Harold Titus

Herculean

Julian wanted to clean his room
but didn't know where to start.
His floor was covered in papers and clothes
and all kinds of bicycle parts.

A **Herculean** effort was needed
to do this **Herculean** task.
"On second thoughts," thought Julian.
"It's really too much to ask!"

Hirsute

Santa Claus is hirsute
with his flowing beard.
If Mrs Santa was hirsute
that might be slightly weird.
And if her *suit* was hirsute
that would be *really* scary
For anything that is **hirsute**
is very, very . . .
HAIRY!

Hyperbole

We tend to use **hyperbole**
a million times a day.
We use it to exaggerate
what we want to say.

For instance, if you say you are
as hungry as a horse . . .
Strictly speaking that would be
impossible of course.

You may complain you're **bored to tears**
but really you're not crying.
You may be **dying for a drink**
but clearly you're not dying.

You swear your backpack **weighs a tonne.**
It doesn't actually—
it's a giant overstatement.
It's hyperbole!

HYPERBOLE PRONUNCIATION ALERT

The way it is written is not how it's heard:
there isn't a **bowl** at the end of the word!

Idiosyncrasy

Different personalities
have different quirks and qualities.
These odd peculiarities
are known as idiosyncrasies.

You might prefer spaghetti cold
or only ever type in **bold.**
Perhaps you like to disagree
and *that's* your idiosyncrasy.

But whether you've a fear of sheep
or love to swim out in the deep,
our every idiosyncrasy
brings individuality.

A TASTY IDOSYNCRASY

The writer Roald Dahl had a peculiar habit. Whenever he ate a bar
of chocolate, he saved the foil. This **idiosyncrasy** may have inspired
Charlie and the Chocolate Factory.

Inconceivable

A man once ate twelve pies at once,
which is unbelievable.
How anyone could eat that much
is simply **inconceivable**.
But then he ate a dozen more.
I can't imagine why.
To me it's **inconceivable**
to be that fond of pie!

"Unthinkable! **Inconceivable!** Absurd!
He could never be made
into marshmallows!"
Charlie and the Chocolate Factory by Roald Dahl

34

Inconspicuous

If you apply to be a spy
be sure you don't stand out.
Don't call attention to yourself.
Don't flap your arms about.

Do not wear a purple wig
or anything ridiculous.
A spy must try to blend right in
they must look inconspicuous.

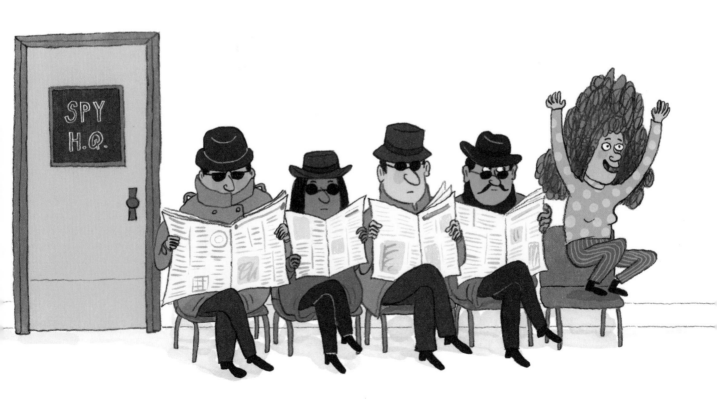

Indisputable

The world's not flat and that is that.
You can't argue.
It's a fact.
The Earth is round as round can be.
It's **indisputable**.
You can't disagree.

Inevitably

Take a big jump
in the deep blue sea,
and you'll get wet **inevitably.**
If you happen to eat
more than you should,
inevitably you won't feel good.
If you get struck by a falling tree,
you'll get squashed **inevitably!**
**As you can see, inevitably is something simply
bound to be.**

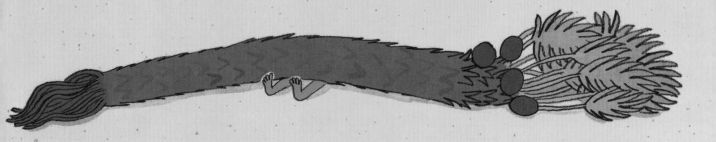

Infinitesimal

If it's smaller than a flea,

a dot or a decimal . . .

If it's *really really* tiny

then it's

infinitesim 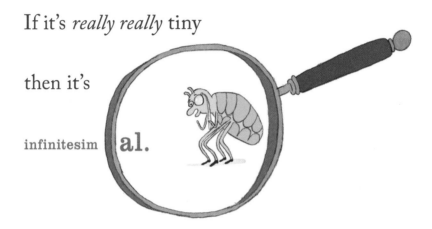 **al.**

> "There was an **infinitesimal**
> pause, just one tiny breath."
>
> *When Dimple Met Rishi* by Sandhya Menon

Iridescent

The color of a bubble
changes in the light.
That **iridescent** quality
is luminous and bright.

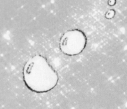

The feathers of a peacock
are **iridescent** blue.
A pearl is **iridescent**
and a dragonfly is too.

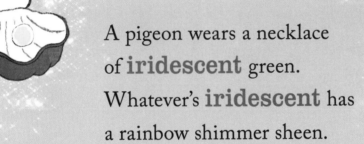

A pigeon wears a necklace
of **iridescent** green.
Whatever's **iridescent** has
a rainbow shimmer sheen.

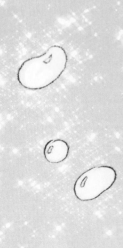

Jovial

A person who is jovial
is happy and outgoing—
Santa Claus is jovial
with all his Ho-Ho-Ho-ing.

By Jove, if someone's jovial
they're chatty and they're jolly.
It's better to be jovial
than miserable,
By Golly!

Judgemental

If you're **judgemental**
you're not open-minded.
You look for fault
where you can find it.

But *if* you're **judgemental**
then here is a fact:
You don't have good judgement.
How funny is that?

> "Be curious, not **judgemental**."
> **Walt Whitman**

Kerfuffle

Princess Puffle had a snuffle,
which set the palace in a **kerfuffle**.
The Maid of the Hanky was summoned at once.
Ten doctors came running and made a big fuss.

Five of them told her to,
"Go straight to bed!"
The other five told her to
stand on her head!

What a commotion.
What a **kerfuffle**.
A right ballyhoo
all because of a snuffle!

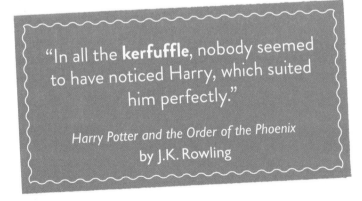

"In all the **kerfuffle**, nobody seemed
to have noticed Harry, which suited
him perfectly."

Harry Potter and the Order of the Phoenix
by J.K. Rowling

Leonine

A **leonine** way of walking
is elegant and proud.
A roar described as **leonine**
would certainly be loud.
The smallest cat is **leonine**
without it even trying.
Whatever may be leonine
is rather like a lion.

Listless

Emily was down in the dumps,
her energy, ever so low.
She couldn't be bothered with anything much.
She'd lost her get up and go.

She wouldn't get dressed or visit with friends.
She simply hadn't an interest.
All she would do is sit on the settee,
droopy and limp and listless.

"Emily dear," her mother implored,
"*why* is it you are so listless?"
"I think it's because," Emily yawned,
"it's 300 days until Christmas."

"But, you see, Jo wasn't a heroine, she was only a struggling human girl like hundreds of others, and she just acted out her nature, being sad, cross, **listless**, or energetic, as the mood suggested."

Little Women
by Louisa May Alcott

Magnanimous

Let's say there's just one piece of cake
and you, in fact, are ravenous.
But still, you give it to your friend
then that would be **magnanimous**.

Or say your mate just won a prize
you felt *you* should have won.
Then it would be **magnanimous**
for you to say, "Well done."

**An act that is magnanimous
is noble and seems effortless.**
There isn't any showy fuss.
It's just quietly generous.

WELL DONE

"I would never have refused anyone who wanted to peek at my answers, I was **magnanimous** with my candy, and I wasn't stuck-up."
The Diary of a Young Girl by Anne Frank

Maxim

A **maxim** is a saying
both concise and true.
It takes a big idea and packs it
in a line or two.

Better safe than sorry.
There's pride before a fall.
A **maxim** makes a line of wisdom
easy to recall.

It takes two to tango.
Look before you leap.
A **maxim** makes a line of wisdom
something you can keep.

What goes around comes round again.
A stitch in time saves nine.
Slow and steady wins the race.
And that's **maxim**, defined!

> "After much thought Snowball declared that the
> Seven Commandments could in effect be reduced to a
> single **maxim**, namely: 'Four legs good, two legs bad.'"
>
> *Animal Farm* by George Orwell

Meander

Please, Amanda don't **meander** on your way back home. You're not to wander here and there—resist the urge to roam. Don't make any extra twists or turns along the way— please, Amanda don't **meander**—hurry home today!

AN ENTERTAINING NOTE

Knock, knock!

    Who's there?

Me and . . .

    Me and who?

Me . . . and . . . 'ER!

Mollified

Molly's out of sorts;

So miffed she nearly cried.

But if you **soothe** and **humor** her
then she'll be **molli**fied.

Nondescript

What can you say about a day
that's **ordinary** in every way:
not bad or good but just **OK**,
a **"nothing special"** kind of day,
so dull that no description fits?
Just say your day was **nondescript!**

Non sequitur

We were talking—
me and you—
all about soccer
when out of the blue—
you suddenly say you like **fishing for trout!**
That's a **non sequitur**—what's that about?
What's trout to do with a soccer pitch?
Does soccer somehow remind you of fish?
All this talk about fish makes me think of . . .
a cup!
?
(That's a second **non sequitur**—please keep up!)

Oblivious

If you went out with your PJ's on
yet didn't seem to notice this . . .
If you'd not seen what was amiss,
you'd be **oblivious** of this.

**When someone's wholly unaware
of something blinking obvious**
that's clear to all the rest of us
then they would be **oblivious**.

> "In a sailboat I become **oblivious**
> to everything else in the world."
> **Albert Einstein**

Onomatopoeia

An onomatopoeia
is a word with a noise inside.
Say the word and you can hear
the sound that it describes.

A **BUZZ** really does make the sound of a buzz

There's a definite drip in **DRIP**

A wind-up clock really goes **TICK TOCK**

And scissors make a **SNIP**

 A hiccup has a hiccup sound

You hear the plop in **PLOP**

RATATATAT sounds just like that

And pop makes a proper  POP!

Ostentatious

Ostentatious tears
are only for display.
They're just a show of misery
that's artfully conveyed.

Ostentatious clothing
sets out to impress.
It calls attention to the wearer:
"See how well I dress!"

An **ostentatious** person
shows off in flashy ways.
"How cool am I? Oh me, oh my!
Please shower me with praise!"

Penultimate

You'll find eight lines inside this rhyme.
The last one is the ultimate.
The one that comes before the last
is known as the penultimate.
Whatever is penultimate
is next to last in line.
And *this* is the **penultimate**
of eight lines in this rhyme!

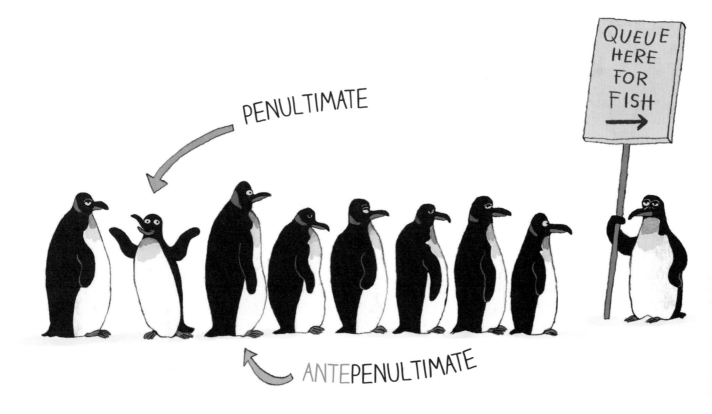

PENULTIMATE

ANTEPENULTIMATE

QUEUE HERE FOR FISH →

AND IN THIRD PLACE . . .

The **antepenultimate** is the one before **penultimate**.

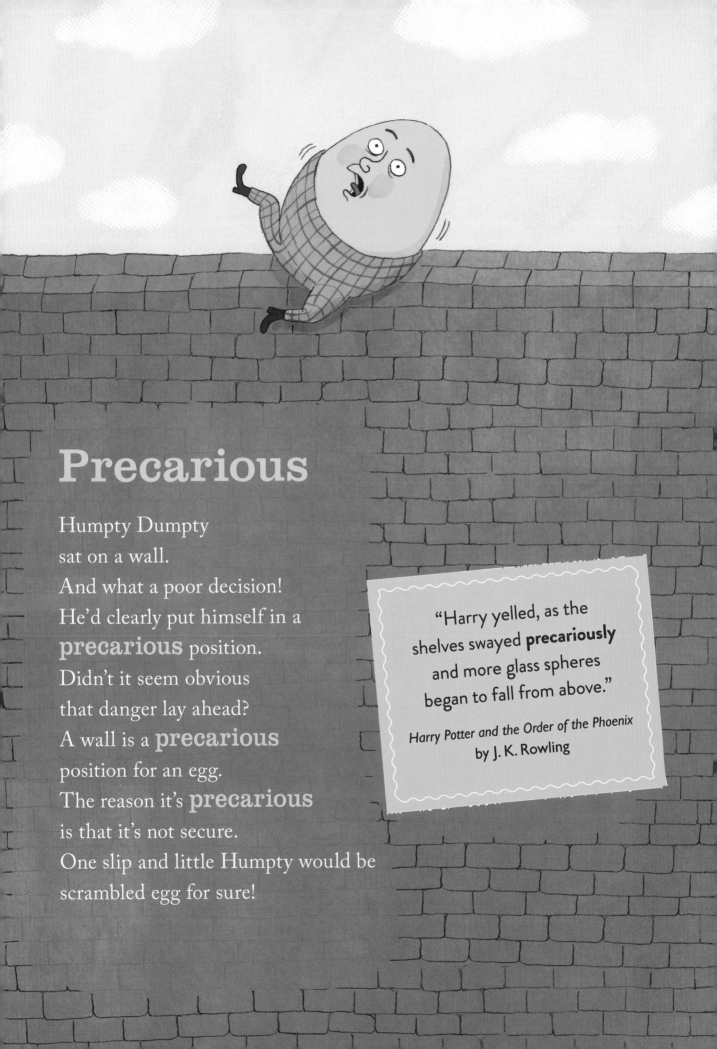

Precarious

Humpty Dumpty
sat on a wall.
And what a poor decision!
He'd clearly put himself in a
precarious position.
Didn't it seem obvious
that danger lay ahead?
A wall is a **precarious**
position for an egg.
The reason it's **precarious**
is that it's not secure.
One slip and little Humpty would be
scrambled egg for sure!

"Harry yelled, as the
shelves swayed **precariously**
and more glass spheres
began to fall from above."

Harry Potter and the Order of the Phoenix
by J. K. Rowling

Procrastinate

Jimmy don't **procrastinate**.
Please clean your room—it's in a state.
Don't put it off—it's getting late.
Jimmy don't **procrastinate**.

Now is *not* the time to start
taking your guitar apart.
It's time to clean your room, I said,
and don't forget to make your bed.

Don't say you'll do it in a bit.
Please will you just get on with it?
Don't tell me you will get round to it.
Don't **procrastinate**—just do it!

Querulous

Little Gus was querulous.
He whined an awful lot.
He complained when it was cold
and when it was too hot.
He'd whinge about his uniform
or having to take the bus.
Little Gus was querulous.
He always made a fuss!
His mother never told him off.
She'd only smile and coo,
"My Gussy Wussy's querulous.
What *can* a mother do?"

WHINGE MASTER

"The little boy, perched behind his father on the broomstick, made one **querulous** comment after another. 'It isn't very comfortable back here. When will we get there? How much longer?"

Harry Potter and the Deathly Hallows by J.K. Rowling

Replete

If you've eaten far too much,
you might say that you feel stuffed.
If you haven't eaten plenty,
you could say that you feel empty.

If what you've had is just enough,
not too little or too much,
but *just* the right amount to eat,
then you could say you feel **replete**.

Retaliate

If somebody calls you an old kangaroo,
you might **retaliate** and call them one too.
If somebody tries to give you a thwack,
you might be tempted to give them one back.
But really you mustn't respond in this way.
No need to **retaliate**—just walk away.

Riveting

It's hard to stop reading
a **riveting** book.
The story is gripping.
You're totally hooked.
You find it compelling.
You're wholly engaged.
A **riveting** book has you
glued to the page!

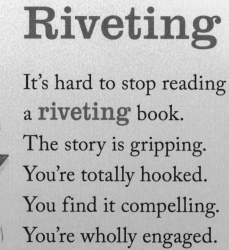

Sanctimonious

Someone **sanctimonious**
believes they are superior.
They do their best to let you know
you're morally inferior.

They like to think they're saintly
and deserve to take a bow—
when someone's sanctimonious
they're holier than thou.

Scintillating

A **scintillating** conversation

sparkles and is captivating

BRIGHT and LIVELY

stimulating

thought provoking.
Elevating.

Soporific

The speech was very boring
and exceptionally long.
The speaker's **soporific** voice
droned on and on and on . . .

And though the people listening
tried hard to stay awake.
Her **soporific** speaking put them
in a drowsy state.

Now and then the speaker stopped
to give a little cough,
not noticing the audience
had gently drifted off!

"I have never felt sleepy after eating lettuces; but then I am not a rabbit. They certainly had a very **soporific** effect upon the Flopsy Bunnies!"

The Tale of the Flopsy Bunnies
by Beatrix Potter

Symbiotic

Jack Sprat could eat no fat.
His wife could eat no lean.
And so between them both you see
they licked the platter clean.

She had the fat, he had the lean,
whenever they had dinner.
**This symbiotic give and take
made each of them a winner**.

Synonymous

You could say *slim*.
Or you could say *thin*.
The two are **synonymous**.
They mean the same thing.

You could say *evening*.
Or you could say *night*.
The two are **synonymous**.
They're very much alike.

You could say *a load of us*.
Or you could say *a lot of us*.
**When words are very similar,
we say they are synonymous.**

Testy

It doesn't take much
to irritate Betsy.
She's annoyed easily.
Betsy is **testy**.

Translucent

Jelly is **translucent**.
Tracing paper too.
When something is **translucent**
just a bit of light comes through.
For example: frosted glass,
apple juice, and beer
are **translucent**, not transparent,
as they're *not completely* clear.

Truculent

**When somebody is truculent,
they're ready for a fight.**
They seem mean and quarrelsome
and might give you a fright.

Someone who is **truculent**
is quick to be defiant.
They tend to argue fiercely and
refuse to be compliant.

They may appear ferocious
and occasionally cruel.
You wouldn't choose a **truculent**
companion, as a rule!

"**Truculently** they squared up to
each other but kept just out of
fighting distance."

Lord of the Flies by William Golding

Unbiased

A teacher can't have favorites.
They must be just and fair.
They shouldn't be especially nice
to people with red hair.

They can't be friendlier to some
or treat one child the highest.
They mustn't favor anyone.
They have to be **unbiased**.

Unruly

They have no discipline at all
the people of the Ghoolie.
They shout and chuck their shoes about.
The Ghoolies are **unruly**!
They won't behave; they pay no mind.
Unmanageable, truly.
They don't like rules of any kind.
The Ghoolies are **unruly**!

Volatile

When somebody is **volatile**
their mood just switches, like a dial:
at first they're nice, then suddenly
they're as mean, as mean can be.

Henry the Eighth was **volatile**.
He'd seem friendly for a while . . .
Then his mood would change instead—
and he'd go chop off someone's head!

Voracious

There was once a tiger
friendly, kind, and gracious.
But still there was this nagging fact
the tiger was **voracious**.
He felt extremely hungry
right from morning until night.
There seemed to be no end to his
voracious appetite.
Then one day, accidentally,
he ate a boy called Lorri.
"I felt **voracious**," said the tiger,
"Now I'm jolly sorry!"

Wily

Artful, Clever, Crafty, Sly,
Scheming, and Designing.
A wily person's all those things.
Plus, Foxy, and Beguiling.

An **EX**planation

Anyone would be perplexed
to find an **Ex** here, not an **X**.
But to be completely truthful
Ex words are a lot more useful!

...QRSTUVW?YZ

The first English Dictionary had no X section – for there
weren't any words beginning with X! Today we have some,
but few, which is why X is usually for "Xylophone" or "X-ray"!

EXhilarated

You can feel **exhilarated**
when you win a race
or if you find your school report
is full of lovely As.
When you feel **exhilarated**
there's an **inner glow**.
You are **thrilled** and **animated**
and you let it show!
The minute you're
exhilarated
there's a sudden
spark.
It's a bit like
swallowing an
exclamation
mark!

"They sped along at a pace that frightened her, but the thunder of their wheels on the hard road and the beat of their scudding feet made her **exhilarated** enough to ignore the discomfort."

The Amber Spyglass by Philip Pullman

Extol

Some **extol** the benefits
of eating loads of kelp.
It's a super food, they say,
a tonic for your health.
Some **extol** the benefits
of standing on your head.
And some **extol** the benefits
of eating cake in bed!

Extortionate

Italian ices are the nicest,
which is most unfortunate.
(We rarely get to have them as
the prices are **extortionate**.)
"They cost the Earth," my mother cries.
"Ten bucks for a cone!
That's a silly kind of price.
Plus, we have ice at home!"

Yearn

You might **yearn** for a puppy.
You might **yearn** for a kiss.
Or maybe you might **yearn** to be
on the Honours list.
When you *really* want something
so much you feel a burn.
**That kind of achy longing
is what it is to yearn.**

"One does not
yearn for that which
is easily acquired."

Ovid

78

Zest

Zest is made from lemon peel.

It gives a cake a **zingy** feel.

Zest is also **energy**.

It's a certain quality.

Say you have a

zest for art—

that means for art,

you have a

spark.

When you do anything with **zest**

you **relish** it and do your best!

"True happiness comes from the joy of deeds well done; the **zest** of creating things new."
Antoine de Saint-Exupéry, author of *The Little Prince*

"Words are the clothes
thoughts wear."

Samuel Beckett